Baby's First Little BOOK of PRAYERS

Wee Witness

Artwork by Billy Attinger

HARVEST HOUSE PUBLISHERS

EUGENE, OREGON

Text Copyright © 2003 by Harvest House Publishers
Published by Harvest House Publishers
Eugene, Oregon 97402

ISBN 0-7369-1185-5

Artwork © by Billy Attinger. Wee Witness® is a registered trademark of Cass
Street Group LP, San Diego, CA and is licensed by Z Strategies, Inc., San Diego,
CA. No part of this book may be reproduced without express written permission.
For licensing information, contact Z Strategies at (619) 543-5193. For information
on other Wee Witness® products, contact Cass Street Group at (877) 432-
1794 or visit us at our web site: www.weewitness.com.

Design and production by Garborg Design Works, Minneapolis, Minnesota

Harvest House Publishers has made every effort to trace the ownership of all
poems and quotes. In the event of a question arising from the use of a poem
or quote, we regret any error made and will be pleased to make the necessary
correction in future editions of this book.

Scriptures quoted from the *International Children's Bible, New Century Version*,
copyright © 1983, 1986, 1988 by Word Publishing, Dallas, Texas 75039.
Used by permission.

Printed in China

05 06 07 08 09 10 / LP / 8 7 6 5 4 3 2

Dear Little One

Love

But Jesus called the little children to him and said to his followers, "Let the little children come to me. Don't stop them, because the kingdom of God belongs to people who are like these little children."

Luke 18:16

Dear Father
who hast all things made,
And carest for them all,
There's none too great
for Your great love,
Nor anything too small.

If You can spend
such tender care
On things that grow so wild,
How wonderful
Your love must be
For me, Your little child.

O heavenly Father, protect and
bless all things that have breath:
Guard them from all evil
and let them sleep in peace.

ALBERT SCHWEITZER

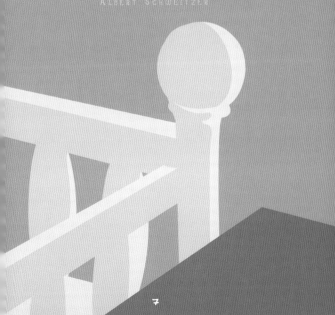

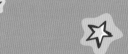

Lord, keep us safe this night,

Secure from all our fears;

May angels guard us while we sleep,

Till morning light appears.

JOHN LELAND

I hear no voice, I feel no touch,
I see no glory bright;
But yet I know that God is near,
In darkness, as in light.

He watches ever by my side,
And hears my whispered prayer;
The Father for His little child
Both night and day doth care.

Now I lay me down to sleep.

I pray the Lord my soul to keep.

May angels watch me through the night

And wake me with the morning light.

18TH CENTURY CHILDREN'S PRAYER

12

What can I give Him,

Poor as I am?

If I were a shepherd,

I would bring Him a lamb;

If I were a wise man,

I would do my part.

But what can I give Him?

Give Him my heart.

CHRISTINA ROSSETTI

I don't need a telephone
To talk to God each day!
When I want to talk to Him,
I close my eyes and pray.

EMILY HUNTER

God sends angels I can't see,

They are watching over me,

Standing by my feet and head,
Angels all around my bed.

Helen Haidle

19

Be near me, Lord Jesus,
I ask Thee to stay
Close by me forever,
and love me, I pray.
Bless all the dear children
in Thy tender care;
And fit us for heaven
to live with Thee there.

MARTIN LUTHER

Now, before I run to play,

Let me not forget to pray

To God who kept me through the night

And waked me with the morning light.

Help me, Lord, to love Thee more

Than I ever loved before,

In my work and in my play,

Be Thou with me through the day.

Amen.

AUTHOR UNKNOWN

Jesus, tender Shepherd, hear me;

Bless Your little lamb tonight;

Through the darkness, please be near me,

Keep me safe till morning light.

All this day Your hand has fed me,

And, I thank You for Your care;

You have warmed me, clothed and fed me,

Listen to my evening prayer.

Let my sins be all forgiven;

Bless the friends I love so well;

Take us all at last to Heaven

Happy there with You to dwell.

MARY DUNCAN

24

A gentle prayer is what I'll say
To close this peaceful, gentle day.
With gratitude that I have heard
The pre-dawn chirpings of a bird.
With thankfulness that I have seen
The many hues of summer green.
With singing heart that I could feel
The soft warm grasses when I kneel.
With love for those who give me care
I softly close my gentle prayer.

27

Thank You for the

world so sweet

Thank You for the

food we eat

Thank You for the

birds that sing

Thank You, Lord, for

everything. Amen.

AUTHOR UNKNOWN

Father in heaven, hear my prayer.

Keep me in Your love and care.

Be my guide in all I do.

Bless all those who love me too. Amen.

Author Unknown

God be in my heart.

God be in my play.

God be in my words and thoughts

Every night and day.

VERONICA CURRIE

GOD

LOVES ME

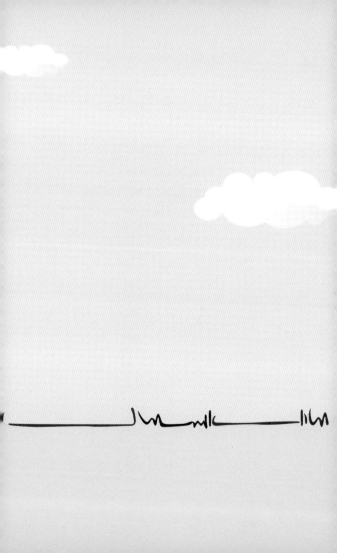